# HOME-BASED BUSINESS IDEAS

10 Easy To Start Businesses
You Can Operate From Home In Your
Pajamas!

By

**Sharron Williams**

# Table of Content

Affiliate Marketer
Bookkeeper/Tax Prepare
Business/Life Coach
E-Commerce
Editorial/Proof Reading Services
Gift Baskets
Translator
Tutor
Virtual Assistant
Webinar/ Teleseminar Host

# INTRODUCTION

Today, more & more individuals are finding themselves out of work and in need of generating an income. Becoming an entrepreneur seems to be the answer for many.

In this publication, you will find 10 low start-up business outlines. For each, an estimated start-up cost, marketing suggestions, related websites and when available any free/low cost training being offered is given. (Note: the names and addresses offered are done so without any guarantees regarding the vendors).

The business outlines in this book are low start-up because they can be started for less than $2000.00 in many cases. One of the best things about these businesses is that you can operate them in your pajamas. They are great for individuals who are home bound & want to have a business or need an income or those caring for family members and employment outside of the home is not possible. Some level of comfort with using a computer & the Internet is a plus. The other skills can be learnt as you go in many cases.

Our goal was to make the information simple yet as complete as possible. We wanted to make it possible for you the reader to put down the book and get started. Before operating your business, you may need a business license, a tax ID# & authorization to collect sales tax. Check with the licensing authority in your county. The outlines are a starting point & a more detailed business plan would be a plus. Checkout our report on "Writing a

Business Plan" by visiting our blog at Williamsauthor.wordpress.com.

Please keep in mind that success is not guaranteed. These outlines are not blueprints to success but rather suggestions on how to implement a particular business. The success you achieve will depend on your commitment, ability and some good fortune from heaven. Good fortune is included because timing is very, very important. If you start the right business at the right time, the possibilities are endless.

Read each outline carefully, some items, which are mentioned throughout the publication, are only explained once. Be sure to write notes for yourself as to your likes and dislikes for a particular venture. Once you have chosen those you like best, go over them and choose the business, which is right for you.

No matter what business you chose, remember to check with your local county and state licensing office to determine if any licenses are needed. Also check with an attorney or accountant if needed.

With the business for you decided, it is time for you to begin. **Start today! Don't wait!! Your financial future is in your hands!!!**

# Affiliate Marketer

## Estimated Start-up Cost:

$500 depending on what equipment you already Own

## Marketing Plan:

Word of Mouth, Website or Blog, Business Cards, Magnetic Car Sign, Offer a Free APP, QR Code, Social Media

## Equipment:

Computer, Misc. Office Supplies, Internet, Digital Camera

## Related Sites:

Clickbank.com, cj.com – both offer free accounts to sell other people's products & receive a commission

Do you enjoy selling but don't have a product to sell? Do you have a way with words? Do you think out side the box? If yes, this may be the business for you.

As an affiliate marketer, you market other people's product for a commission. For best results, it is better to have one website per product theme. For example, if you are selling exercise equipment, don't sell exercise cloths on the same site. Direct them to another site. By doing this, you are better able to use key words, which will bring customers to your site when they search for the specific topic.

When developing your marketing plan, make sure you clearly understand who your potential customers are. This is important because you want them to find you and therefore your keywords are important.

Keywords are the words you associate with your website which allows your website to be found when the words are searched on the Internet. Your keywords should be use throughout your site for example, in the product description.

You should be familiar with products you sell. This is important because you want to create a compelling description with words, which will turn the visitor into a customer. I believe the best way to achieve this is to be familiar with the product which allows you to give a testimonial.

Your potential customer is looking for an assurance that this product will meet his or her need. Your glowing testimonial will help them say yes. Please make sure you write only the truth because you want customers for life who will refer you to their friends. If what you say about the product is not what is experienced after the purchase, you have lost a customer.

In affiliate marketing, your reputation is of great value. When potential customers hear your name associated with a product, you want the reputation of "If you say it is good, I believe it". Protect your reputation by never promising a product will do something it will not.

One of the ways to sell products as an affiliate is by writing an article on a blog or website. Let's stick with selling exercise equipment, first you would decide if you want to feature one or more items in the article. (Note: I suggest not more than three to keep the article short enough for people to read easily). Next you would choose the items, keeping in mind any theme you may have. For example, you may want to write about upper body workout. With this in mind, you may choose an equipment which works the arms, and then another which worked on the chest. After choosing your products, it is time to write the article.

Now create the most compelling description of the benefits of using these products as you can, using words. You want the potential buyer to know exactly what to expect. I suggest writing the article as if you were telling a friend about some great thing you discovered.

Throughout the article, have links to the seller's product page, which will usually has more information and purchasing details.

You may be wondering how you will get paid. Good question. After you sign up at an affiliate site, you will be able to choose the product you want to sell or promote. When a product is chosen, you are assigned an affiliate code, which can be in the form of an URL and will direct potential buyers from your site to the seller's product page. The

URL contains your code, which informs the seller that you referred a particular buyer. Once a purchase is made, your commission is credited to your account.

Payment of your commission will not be made immediately. Time is allowed for the buyer to return the product and certain dollar thresholds usually have to be met. Most companies will not pay commissions on amounts less than $10.00; other $50.00 and some are even higher.

What is good about affiliate marketing is once you set up the site, it is working for you 24/7. You will need to monitor the site to determine its effectiveness. One site will probably not make you a millionaire but with a few well producing sites, you should do well.

# Bookkeeper/Tax Prepare

### Estimated Start-up Cost:

$900 (Depending on the equipment you already have)

### Marketing Plan:

Word of Mouth, Website or Blog, Business Cards, Magnetic Car Sign, Offer a Free APP, QR Code, Social Media, Brochure

### Equipment:

Computer, Phone, Contact Management Software, Tax Software, Bookkeeping software, Misc. Office Supplies, Internet, e-Fax

### Related Sites:

Skype.com-provides free video calling to other Skype users. PayPal, Google cart or other shopping cart

Do you enjoy working with numbers; do you have an accounting degree? If you do, this may be the business for you.

Tax preparation is a seasonal business but add bookkeeping and you have a year round business. Many small businesses need and want the services of a reliable, accurate, bookkeeper with integrity. If you are not comfortable with the tax code, then offering only bookkeeping services may be for you.

You will keep your customer's records in good order for them to use at tax time.

With all the bookkeeping and tax preparation software available, you should be able to find one, which you are comfortable using.

Your customers can drop off their paperwork, scan and e-mail them, e-fax them or send them by mail to you. You may not be able to have customers come to your home for a consultation so the consultation can be done over the phone, the Internet using Skype, or by e-mail. If you cannot leave your home to meet them or have them come to you, it is still doable, especially if you provide top-notch customer service.

Keep in mind that dealing with other people's money has its own set of challenges. People are very protective about their finances-as they should be. If you present yourself as a reliable, expert with integrity and discretion, your customers will have confidence in you, which is vital to your success.

In marketing your business, you may want to stress the fact that because everything is done via the Internet, costs are kept at a minimum. Asking for and rewarding referrals, should also be a major component. Word of mouth is your best marketing tool. You can reward existing clients who refer new clients by giving them a reduction on a service or treating them to lunch with a gift card.

Now keep in mind, when you first start, you may need to meet with potential customers to sell them on you and your business. People need to feel comfortable with anyone dealing with their money. Again, stress the fact that because you operate over the Internet they save because it reduces paper, postage, and travel time and the savings is being passed on to them.

The main purpose of a marketing plan is to let people know of your existence. The suggestions given above are by no means engraved in stone. If you have others ideas you prefer and have proven to be successful for you, please don't hesitate to use them. Remember, stress the level of professionalism you can and will provide.

# Business/Life Coach

### Estimated Start-up Cost:

$500 (Depending on the equipment you already have)

### Marketing Plan:

Word of Mouth, Website or Blog, Business Cards, and Magnetic Car Sign, Offer a Free APP, QR Code, Social Media, Joint Ventures, E-mail Campaign

### Equipment:

Computer, Phone, Contact Management Software or File Folders, Web cam, Misc. Office Supplies, Internet, Microphone

### Related Sites:

School of Coaching Mastery web link
http://www.schoolofcoachingmastery.com/free-coachtrainingprogra/
they offer a
free training program. Expertrating.com offers a certification programs at a reasonable price. PayPal, Google or other shopping cart

Business/Life coaches are becoming more and more in demand as individuals realize the need for help in taking their life and careers to the next level. Coaches provide insight and accountability. If people are always coming to you for advice, this may be the business for you.

Although you do not need a certification to become a life coach, having one will give you some credibility when you are first starting out. The school offering the free training program also offers access to free study groups which allows you to gain experience and keep honing the skills already in place by taking turns leading the study group

The classes are offered online which allows you to work at your own pace. To become certified, you must become a member of the school. Visit the site for details.

Developing a good website is probably the best thing you can do for your business. On every printed ad you distribute, should contain your web address for them to visit to get more detailed information about your business. Your website will work for you 24/7 if promoted correctly. Try searching for free websites, which will keep your start-up costs low. Some free sites are weebly.com and yola.com which offer easy to build do-it-yourself websites.

You can get free business cards from vistaprint.com-you pay shipping & processing. Try to make them as unique as possible. You want your card to stand out when you give it to some one.

Another great tool is a car magnet. They can be used to direct people to your website, as well as, tell people about your business while they are stopped at a traffic light, waiting in traffic, or parked on the street. Like a website, the magnets are constantly working for you. Vistaprint.com offers door magnets at a reasonable price-check them out.

Offering a free app to your website which lists your products and services will allow you to tap into the mobile market. Cell phones are making home phones obsolete & an app allows you to market to them effectively. You can build your app for free at appmakr.com, appsbar.com, theappbuilder.com. Dudamobile.com will make your website mobile friendly for free.

Create a QR code to direct potential customers with smart phones to your website and products. This can be done for free at goo.gl (when you shorten your website's URL, a QR code is automatically generated) or delivr.com. Put your code on your Facebook page and all advertising.

In addition to Facebook, consider Twitter, Pinterest and Linken as part of your social media marketing.

When developing your marketing plan, remember to keep in mind who your customers are and where they are most likely found. You may want to specialize in a certain area. For example, you may be a business coach who helps owners take their business to the next level or a personal coach to help stuck people move forward. You may want to help people re-entering to the job market or those retiring and are unsure of the future. Narrowing your focus will help make your marketing more effective.

Decide on your hours of operation and stick to it. You are a professional who happens to work from home some structure is needed. You may decide to work only in the morning hours or only in the evening or a combination of both. This will be determined by the other activities in your life.

If possible create a dedicated area for your business. When using the web cam, keep the background simple as not to detract from the session. At all times there should be no loud noises, these are your paying or potentially paying customers and they expect a professional atmosphere.

Some customers may prefer to conduct their sessions via the phone, while others prefer using a web cam and the Internet so be flexible.

Please remember this is a service business and as such, the quality of the service you provide is very, very important. When dealing with your customers you must develop a rapport. Make your customer feel confident in you. *YOU ARE A RELIABLE PROFESSIONAL!* As always, promise less and deliver more! **Referrals from satisfied customers are always the best form of advertising.**

# E-Commerce

## Estimated Start-up Cost:

$500 or less depending on what equipment you already own

## Marketing Plan:

Word of Mouth, Website or Blog, Business Cards, Magnetic Car Sign, Offer a Free APP, QR Code, Social Media

## Equipment:

Computer, Misc. Office Supplies, Internet, Digital Camera

## Related Sites:

Clickbank.com & cj.com – both offer free accounts to sell other people's products for a commission. Internationalwholesale.com & Dollardays.com are wholesalers, which allow you to purchase products for re-sale. Services.amazon.com and Mp.barnesandnoble.com both allow you to sell products on their website and pay them a fee. Paypal.com, Google or other shopping cart

Do you enjoy selling? Have an idea for a product. This business may be for you. The Internet is the global marketplace, which allows everyone to participate at a relatively low cost.

If you have a product to sell or have dreamt of owning your own retail business, but the start-up costs were too high, selling on the Internet may be your answer.

To get started, you will need a website and clear good quality pictures of your product. If you will be re-selling, the manufacturer usually provides pictures of the product. If you are selling your own product, be sure your picture does the product justice. Using a black or a white background is usually helpful when taking the product photos.

Depending on how you structure this business, you will most likely need permission from your state department of revenue to collect sales tax. I say depending because if you place your products on a website which will process the sale, they usually also collect the sales tax and remit it to the appropriate authority. Before placing your products on any third party website, determine who is responsible for collecting and remitting the sales tax.

When planning your marketing strategy, keep in mind that your business will be competing with every other business of its kind on the internet. Therefore you must choose keywords that will help your website appear on the first page, if not, then the second page, when your topic is searched. "Why" you may ask. Another good question!

The answer is because; most people do not look further than the first few pages of a search result. Therefore, you want to have your website viewed by appearing as close to the top, if not at the top of your search category, keywords help with this.

If you don't mind advertising on your car, a bumper sticker, or car magnet is great tool because they can be easily removed if needed. These are great because as you drive around doing your errands, you are advertising your business. Think about it, in traffic, at stop lights and in parking lots your car is working to help generate business.

A great tool to capture the mobile savvy buyer is to include a QR code on all you printed ads. This would include your car magnet or bumper sticker. The QR code, allows users of Smartphone quick access to your information. You would link the code to a page on your website.

Offering a free app is another great tool for capturing the mobile user market. There are websites which allow you to create apps or you can have it done for you by a professional. Now once someone visits your website, you would give them the opportunity to get your free app. By offering your app, you are making it easy for them to revisit you. The more they visit, the more opportunity you have to sell them something.

If you like using social media, consider creating a business profile. Once created, invite people to join your community. You can offer discounts, free items, and monthly giveaways to name a few suggestions. Building your community allows you to create a ready pool of potential customers for future products.

# Editorial/Proof Reading Services

### Estimated Start-up Cost:

$500 (Depending on the equipment you already have)

### Marketing Plan:

Word of Mouth, Website or Blog, Business Cards, Magnetic Car Sign, Offer a Free APP, QR Code, Social Media, Brochure, Forums, Pay per click ads

### Equipment:

Computer, Phone, Contact Management Software, Misc. Office Supplies, Internet, e-Fax

### Related Sites:

PayPal, Google or other shopping cart

Do you enjoy reading? Are you well verse in spelling and grammar? If yes, then this business might be for you.

With the rise of independent authors, the need for independent editors and proofreaders has also risen. Amazon and Barnes and Noble have made it possible for anyone to become a published author through there digital and print-on-demand mediums. Some individuals prefer not to do everything themselves, for example, editing/proofing their work.

Now please keep in mind that a person's work is very dear to them and if you are hired as a proofer, you are only required to correct spelling, grammar and punctuation. You are not required to give your opinion about the plot or the characters; this is what the editor does.

If you are hired to perform editorial services, again please keep in mind that when critiquing the work, the author has a great deal invested in it and usually feels the work is publishing worthy. Be honest but courteous when conveying your thoughts. You want the reputation of someone who is a professional. Referrals are a great form of marketing and you should strive to earn them.

Whatever service you provide, confidentiality is very important. Potential customers must feel you are trustworthy. Don't be surprised or insulted if they ask you to sign a confidentiality agreement before working with you. As a matter of fact, you should automatically include one in your service agreements.

Let us talk a little about the service agreement/contract. Any agreement/contract should state all terms agreed upon. Never assume anything. Check online for sample contracts and speak with an attorney. Making sure all the "I's" are dotted and the "T's" are crossed in the beginning saves a lot of heartache later.

Participating in writing forums, pay per click ads, your website along with a car magnet are ways you can market your service.

Your customers can send you their work by fax, email or e-fax. As often as possible, try to complete the job early. Do not sacrifice accuracy for speed.

Check the market to see what others providing similar services are charging. To receive payment for your services, you will need to add a shopping cart to your website. Both PayPal and Google offer a pay as you go shopping cart plan. Check them out to see if they meet your needs. There are other companies which offer shopping cart services so comparison shop to find the one that is right for you.

# Gift Baskets

## Estimated Start-up Cost:

$2,000 (Depending on the equipment you already have & products for basket)

## Marketing Plan:

Word of Mouth, Website or Blog, Business Cards, Magnetic Car Sign, Offer a Free APP, QR Code, Social Media, Brochure

## Equipment:

Computer, Phone, Billing Software, Misc. Office Supplies, Internet, e-Fax

## Related Site:

Dollardays.com- wholesaler of various products includes closeouts. Internationalwholesale.com – of various products. Both companies allow you to create free accounts. PayPal, Google or other shopping cart

If you are creative and enjoy putting things together in a unique way, this business might be for you.

This can be operated from home without ever having to leave. The wholesalers provided have their products online and will ship to you. You in turn, once your baskets are created will ship them to your customer and with the US postal service willing to pick up your items and ship at a flat rate depending on the package size, you truly need not leave your home to operate this business.

Your online presents-website or blog, must have clear sharp pictures which represent the actual product. The description should also be clear and easy to understand. Your customer should be wowed when they open their package.

Try to use unique re-usable containers to hold the other items. Pack the items as not to become damaged during shipment.

Before beginning, determine what type of gift baskets you will sell. Will they be gourmet baskets, theme oriented i.e. little princes or tough cowboy, or reasonably price variety baskets.

What is your market? Will you have baskets for every holiday only or will you also carry special occasion baskets as well i.e. birthday, graduation ect. Who are your customers and where are they located? For example, will you have corporate clients, individual clients or both? Are you going after a certain age group?

Be sure to make ordering your product, as easy as possible. Give your customer ordering options, for example by phone, fax or online.

Develop a brochure to give to potential customers. Making sure your QR code is on it directing them to your website.

Pinertest is a great social medium for this type of business. Pin your products to theme boards and don't forget to add a description. You are only limited by your imagination!

Try thinking outside the box when developing your business. For example, you may want to have a basket of the month club which can be given as a gift and would give you a monthly income. Each month could have a different theme to keep things interesting. Also consider having local shops sell your gift baskets and offering gift baskets to order based on your inventory.

Creativity is a key element in this business.

# Translator

## Estimated Start-up Cost:

$500 (Depending on the equipment you already have)

## Marketing Plan:

Word of Mouth, Website or Blog, Business Cards, Magnetic Car Sign, Offer a Free APP, QR Code, Social Media

## Equipment:

Computer, Phone, Contact Management Software or File Folders, Misc. Office Supplies, Internet, e-Fax,

## Related Sites:

Odesk.com & Translatorstown.com are both free job-posting sites; Translatorscafe.com is a social site, which also offers free postings. PayPal or other shopping cart

In today's multi-cultural, society, individuals fluent in a second language are in demand. Various organizations need them to assist them in doing business globally. For example, companies need them as customer service reps, and authors need them to translate their work to reach more markets. If you enjoy reading and speak a second language, this business might be for you.

What is great about this business is it can be done any time of the day. Once you get a job and the due date, it is up to you when you actually do the work. You rarely have interaction with your customer until the completion unless you need some clarification & this can be handled by email.

Consider Facebook, Pinterest & Linken for your social media marketing.

As always over deliver, by completing the job early and in a professional manner. Word of mouth is the best referral.

To get started, visit a free posting site and create a free profile. See what others are charging to help determine your price. Always respond to an inquire quickly & professionally. Remember there are others who want the job and most likely you are not the only one being contacted.

As stated elsewhere, a website or blog, and car magnets are great forms of advertising because they work 24/7. Offering a free app which links to your website or blog and using QR codes will allow you to capture the mobile market.

You want to consider creating a flier or brochure to distribute to local businesses offering to translate for them. i.e. translate a restaurant's menu into another language to help increase there customer base.

I cannot state enough, always be professional which means you keep things confidential and get things done on time!

# Tutor

## Estimated Start-up Cost:

$500 or less depending on what equipment you
already have

## Marketing Plan:

Word of Mouth, Website or Blog, Business Cards,
Magnetic Car Sign, Offer a Free APP, QR Code,
Brochure or Flier, Social Media

## Equipment:

Computer, Phone, Web cam, Misc. Office Supplies,
Internet, Microphone

## Related sites:

Tutoring-expert.com allows you to post a free
profile for jobs, visit site for details. Skype.com has
free video calling PayPal, Google or other shopping
cart,

If you are a teacher or college student proficient in a
particular subject, this might be the business for
you.

Once you have developed a website or blog and
have an online profile, create a flier or brochure to
distribute to local schools and universities. Stress
the convenience of online tutoring-it is flexible &
does not require travel time. Talk about your
knowledge of the subject and mention any awards
you may have received. Make sure your QR code is

on all your printed marketing material.(Note: Your QR code must be large enough to be read at least one and a half inches should do it but always test the code to make sure it works.)

If possible create a dedicated area for your business. When using the web cam, keep the background simple as not to detract from the session. At all times there should be no loud noises, these are your paying or potentially paying customers and they expect a professional atmosphere.

Check in your area for the going rates charged. You may want to consider charging a little less than the going rate in the beginning until you get established. Please do not give away your time and knowledge by charging too little. Your time and knowledge are valuable and you deserve to be properly compensated for them.

You may want to consider building a community by offering time each month where the student can ask questions and get clarification on items. These would not be tutoring sessions; instead they would be a time for questions and answers. This service could supplement the tutoring. For example, a person could pay $20/mo to be able to email you up to ten questions/mo.

Building a referral business should be a goal. I can not say it enough; word of mouth is the best form of advertising. Be Professional, go the extra mile by giving a little more than promised and you should gain referrals.

# Virtual Assistant

## Estimated Start-up cost:

$800 (Depending on the equipment you already have)

## Marketing Plan:

Word of Mouth, Website or Blog, Business Cards, Magnetic Car Sign, Offer a Free APP, QR Code, Attend Local Networking Events, Social Media

## Equipment:

Computer, Phone, Contact Management Software, Web cam, Misc. Office Supplies, Internet, e-Fax

## Related Sites:

Virtualassistantforums.com & Vanetworking.com both allow you to set up free profiles. Expertrating.com offers a certification course at a reasonable price. PayPal or other shopping cart. Skype.com

If you have great administrative skills, this might be the business for you. Virtual assistants (VA for short) are becoming more and more in demand as companies reduce cost by hiring these independent contractors. They are hired on both long and short-term basis by Realtors, business/life coaches and attorneys just to name a few.

Before beginning, take a true assessment of the skills you are bringing to the table. Determine who would benefit the most from them and where they are located. Choose your niche and direct your marketing towards it. Within your niche, you may want to specialize in an area or two.

Facebook, Twitter, Pinterest and Linken should be apart of your social media marketing.

When setting a price for your services in the beginning, again I suggest you see what others are charging in your niche for similar services and let that be your guide.

Technology is very important to this business. Your customers must be able to contact you &/or get information to you during the agreed upon hours. An e-fax is a great tool because faxes are sent to your e-mail, which allows you to be out of your office and still receive documents.

Check online for sample contracts and as always I suggested contacting an attorney to have templates made for you.

Virtual assistants can perform a variety clerical and administrative of services and therefore some have chosen to specialize in specific area, while others specialize in a specific industry. You may want to determine a list of services or you may want to negotiate with each customer based on their individual needs.

Your major selling point should be your reliability and professionalism.

# Webinar/ Teleseminar Host

### Estimated Start-up Cost:

$500 (Depending on what equipment you already have)

### Marketing Plan:

Website or Blog, Business Cards, Offer a Free APP, QR Code, Referrals, Joint Ventures, Social Media, E-mail

### Equipment:

Computer, Phone, Web cam, Microphone, Misc. Office Supplies, Internet

### Related Sites:

Anymeeting.com – offers free webinars & conferences for up to 200 attendees, who can also by phone. PayPal or other shopping cart

Are you an expert in a field? Have you written a book and want to go to the next level? Then becoming a webinar / teleseminar host may be for you.

By packaging your knowledge into a seminar held on the Internet, you leverage your-self and your income in a positive manner. Webinars allow you to bring information to your customers in a convenient way, which increases the attendance rate. Think about it. You can schedule a one hour seminar at 9pm in the evening which allows would be participants to complete needed daily tasks before attending & they attend in the comfort of their homes.

Facebook is a great social media to use with this type of business. As the seminar is going, you can direct participants to your Facebook page to ask questions and leave comments. This is a great way to build a community of potential customers.

Twitter is a great way to send out blasts about your event as well as give updates.

When starting out, you may not be comfortable speaking on a topic for an hour but you could interview a subject matter expert or joint venture with others. What is great is that most web-hosting companies will record the webinar for you, which you can offer to your customers once the webinar ends.

You may have a live feed meaning the participants are watching presenters in real time in front of the camera speaking, or have a power point presentation or a still picture, i.e. of the lecturers, on the screen for the participants to view as they listen

Webinars and teleseminars are a great way to reach a large number of people at one time. For best results, you should offer a free content fill seminar and then a product or service at the end for purchase.

The convenience and saving of travel time and money is making webinars and teleseminars very,

very popular. Not only do the participants attend from the comfort of their home but would be guests can also be interviewed from the comfort of their home-depending on the hosting plan. Wow!!

On the previous pages, we have presented to you businesses, which can be started with relatively little capitol. We have also made suggestions on how to market your business, and provided links to other relevant sites whenever possible. As you were reading, you should have been writing down your comments and by now you should have an idea which business or businesses are right for you.

Anyone with a desire to become an entrepreneur can do so with one of these businesses without much previous training. They are also good for many different ages. Young adults seeking to become entrepreneurs can also start some of these businesses.

Deciding which business is for you is step one on your way to achieving your financial goals. Step two involves creating a business plan (which can be purchased from us). This plan would include a marketing program that fits your product, as well as budget. The suggestions we have made through out this publication have been low cost and by now means are they your only means of advertising. They were given as a starting point.

Websites were suggested through out this book as a form of advertising, because they allow you to give details about your business or service at a low cost. One of the best things about a website is it works even when you are sleeping.

The sources for training, possible associations and other related websites have been provided only as suggested starting point. Do your own homework and locate other sources. Make sure what they are offering fits with your goals.

Choosing a business entity is also very important. The topic needed to be discussed in detail so we suggest you do investigation or purchase our "How to write a Business Plan" in it we discuss the pros and cons of various business entities. Most people start as a sole proprietor but the amount of liability you will expose yourself and your family to may dictate the use of another entity.

Starting a business is not easy and no guarantees exist for success. Once you've made your decision to take control of your financial future, *you **must act***. Don't analyze your business to death. Your final steps are to make sure you have a sound business plan, to get all the professional advice you need, and to go ahead and start. **You deserve financial security.**

www.ingramcontent.com/pod-product-compliance
Lightning Source LLC
Chambersburg PA
CBHW071554170526
45166CB00004B/1660